Explore Rockets

Lola Schaefer

Lerner Publications ◆ Minneapolis

Lerner Publications Company
An imprint of Lerner Publishing Group, Inc.
241 First Avenue North
Minneapolis, MN 55401 USA

For reading levels and more information, look up this title at www.lernerbooks.com.

Main body text set in Billy Infant Regular. Typeface provided by SparkType.

Library of Congress Cataloging-in-Publication Data

Names: Schaefer, Lola M., 1950- author.
Title: Explore rockets / Lola M. Schaefer.
Description: Minneapolis, MN : Lerner Publications Company, an imprint of Lerner Publishing Group, Inc., [2023] | Series: Lightning bolt books. Exploring space | Includes index. | Audience: Ages 6-9. | Audience: Grades 2-3. | Summary: "Readers will learn about the history of rockets, how rockets work, how we may use rockets in the future, and more in this exciting exploration of these essential space machines!"— Provided by publisher.
Identifiers: LCCN 2021037883 | ISBN 9781728457789 (lib. bdg.) | ISBN 9781728463452 (pbk.) | ISBN 9781728461564 (EB pdf)
Subjects: LCSH: Rockets (Aeronautics)—Juvenile literature.
Classification: LCC TL782.5 .S33 2023 | DDC 621.43/56—dc23/eng/20211007

LC record available at https://lccn.loc.gov/2021037883

Manufactured in the United States of America
1-50806-50145-10/21/2021

Table of Contents

Blastoff!

Three, two, one . . . liftoff! Engines burn fuel. Hot gas and smoke billow across the ground. Flames burst from the bottom of the rocket.

Burning fuel makes a force called thrust. Thrust pushes the rocket away from Earth. It soars through the sky and into space.

The Story of Rockets

The first rockets were tubes filled with gunpowder. When lit, they flew sideways. These rockets were used in war.

Robert Goddard made the first rocket that burned fuel in 1926. The scientist dreamed that a rocket would one day fly to the moon.

On October 4, 1957, the space age began. A rocket carried Sputnik 1, the first satellite made by humans, into space. The satellite orbited Earth for ninety-eight minutes.

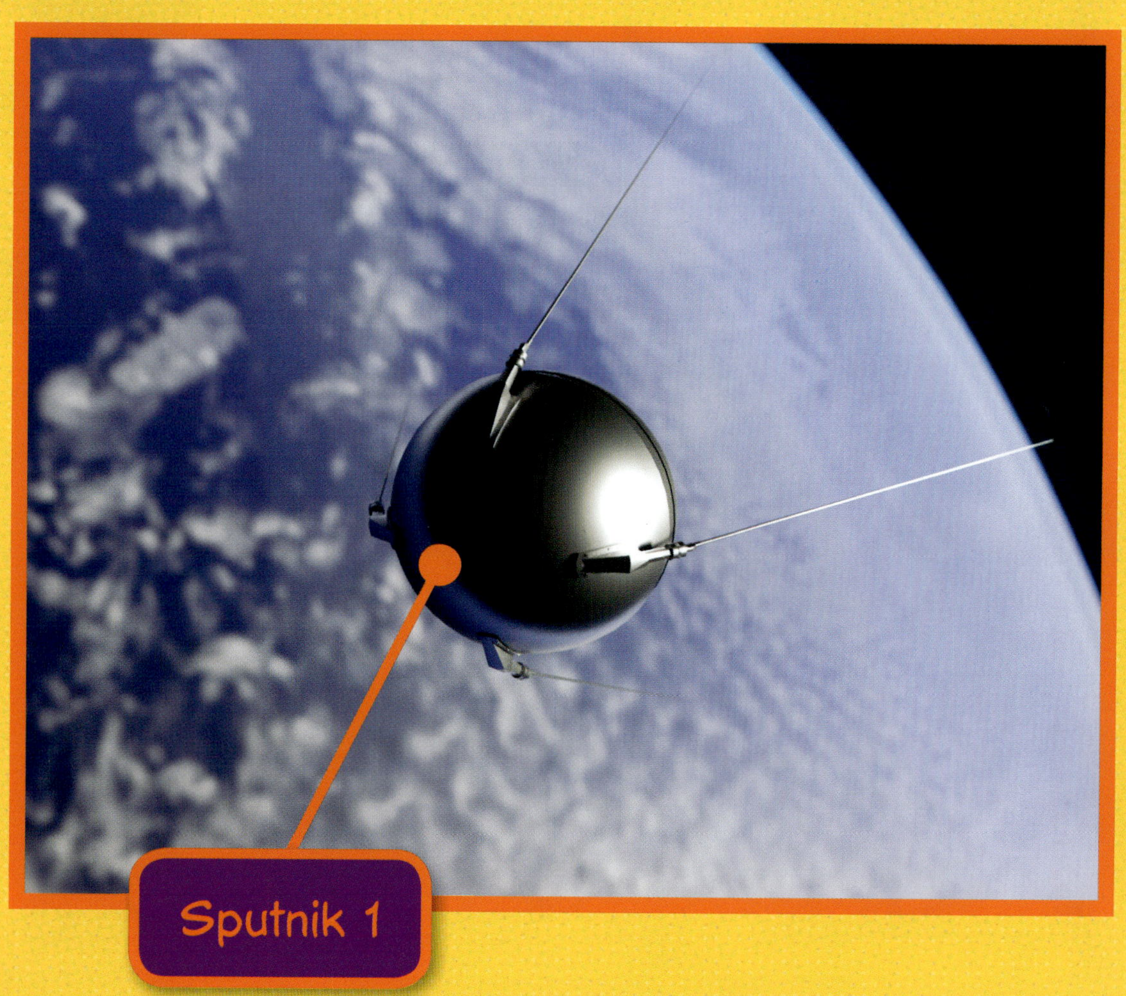

The first rockets did not have people on them. But soon, astronauts flew into space. They orbited Earth and sent information to scientists about all they saw and did.

Astronauts safely left their capsules while in space. Some worked on their spacecraft. Others did experiments. **Astronauts even walked on the moon!**

The first rockets were used only once. Soon scientists made spacecraft that could leave Earth and return. These were used again and again.

Rockets in Action

During liftoff, fuel mixes with oxygen and explodes in a rocket's engine. The burning fuel comes out of the nozzle. This pushes the rocket away from Earth.

A rocket has to travel very fast to enter space. It travels nearly three hundred times faster than a car travels on a highway!

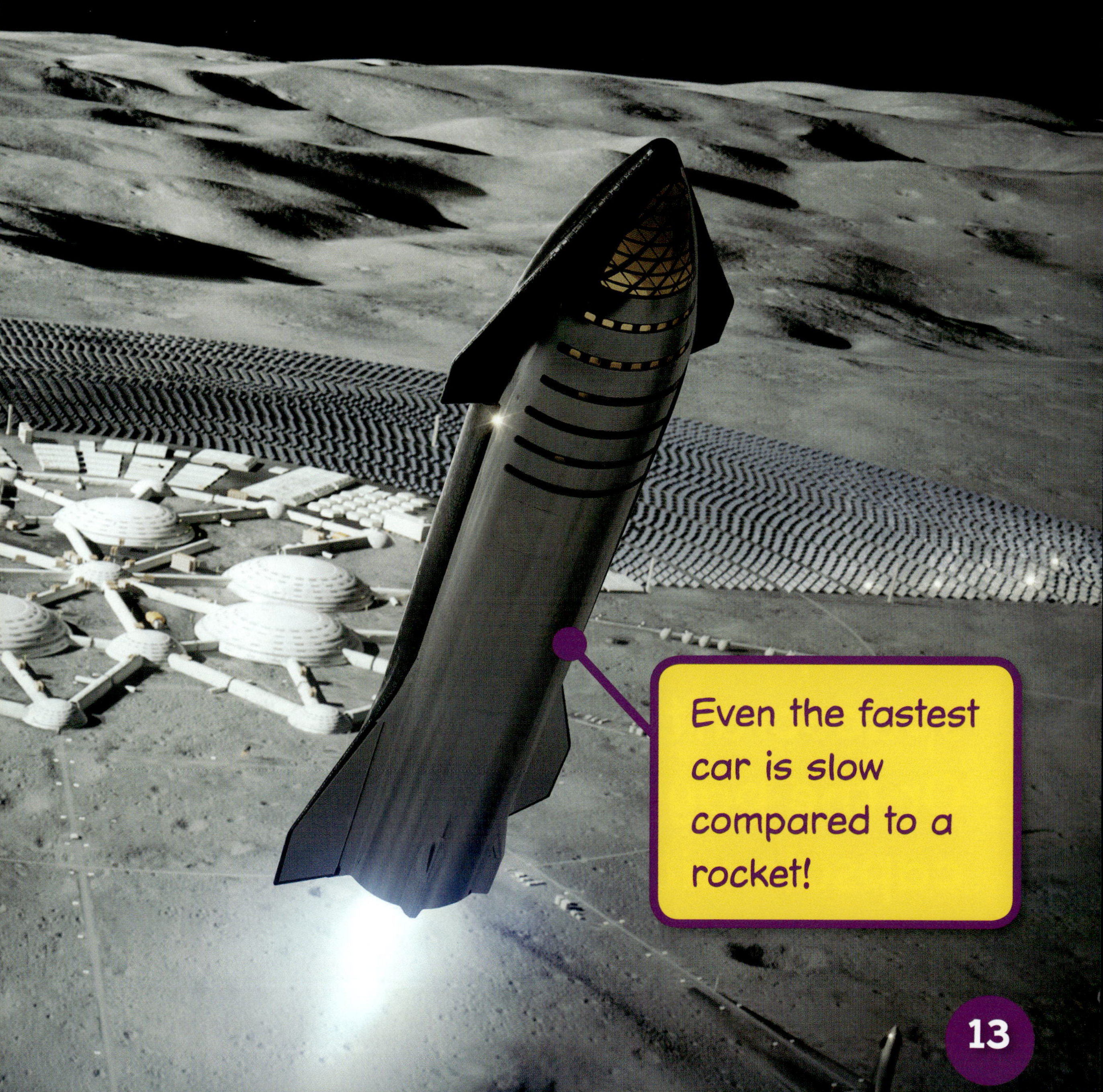

A rocket takes a payload into space. This might be a spacecraft such as a satellite. Or the payload could be a capsule with astronauts and their tools.

Some rockets carry machines that land and then move across the moon or other planets. These are rovers.

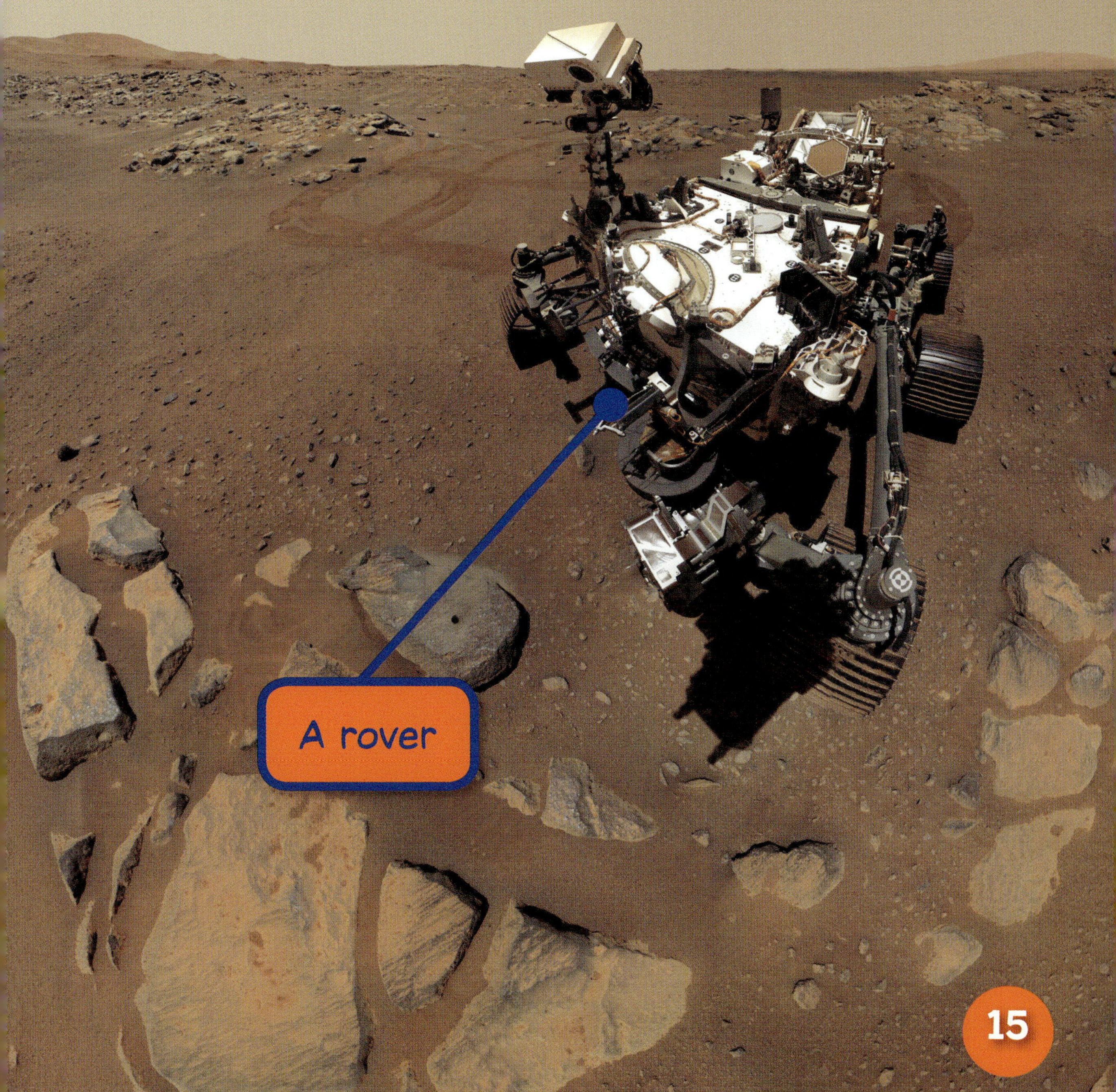

Into the Unknown

Scientists want to know what is beyond our moon and planets. They are sending rockets and spacecraft farther and farther into space.

Newer rockets will weigh less and fly faster. They will use cleaner fuels.

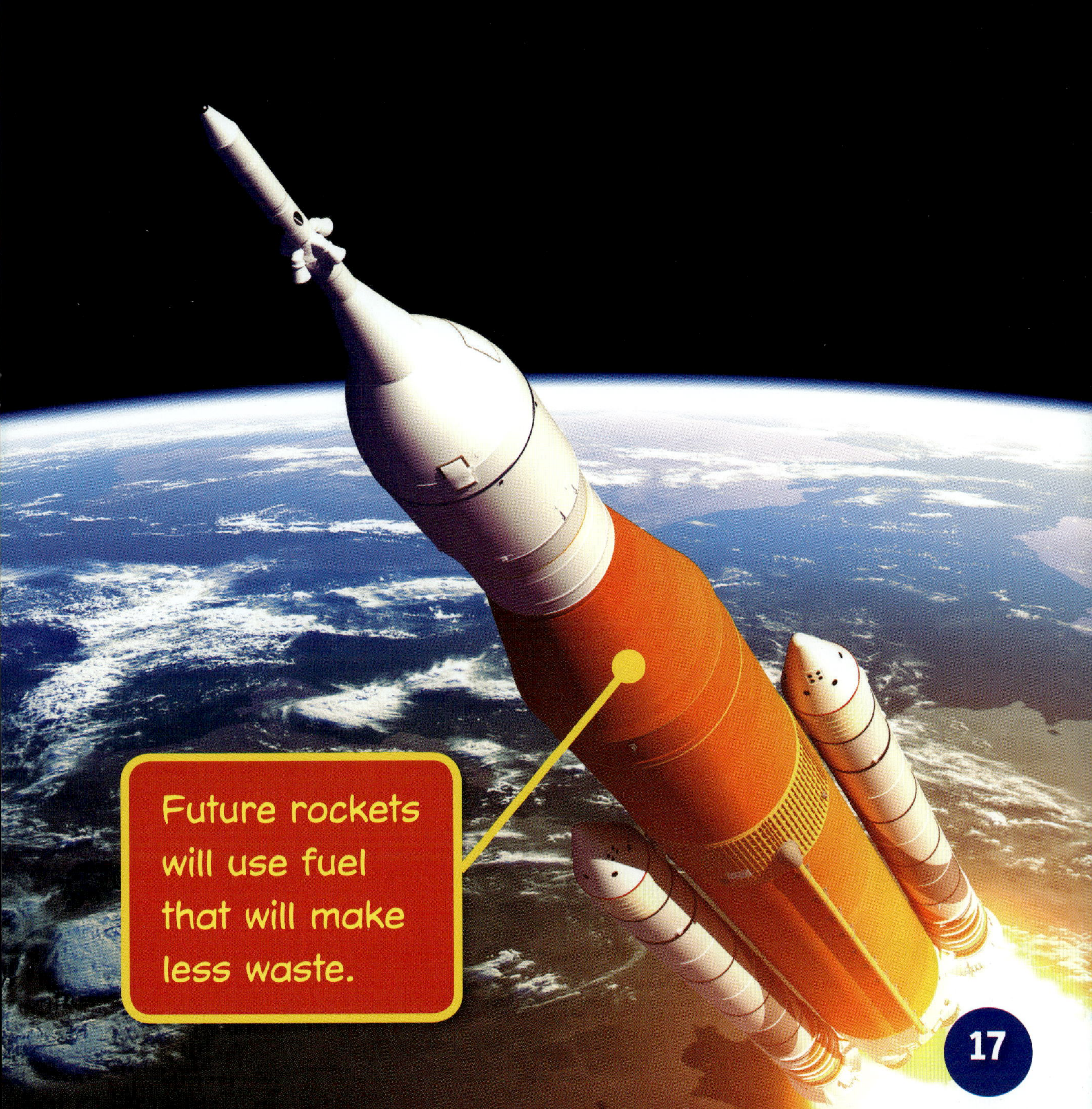

One day, people may fly in rockets for fun. **They may sleep in space hotels!**

People have explored only a small part of space. There will be more to discover for many years. Maybe one day you will find something new in space!

Rocket Diagram

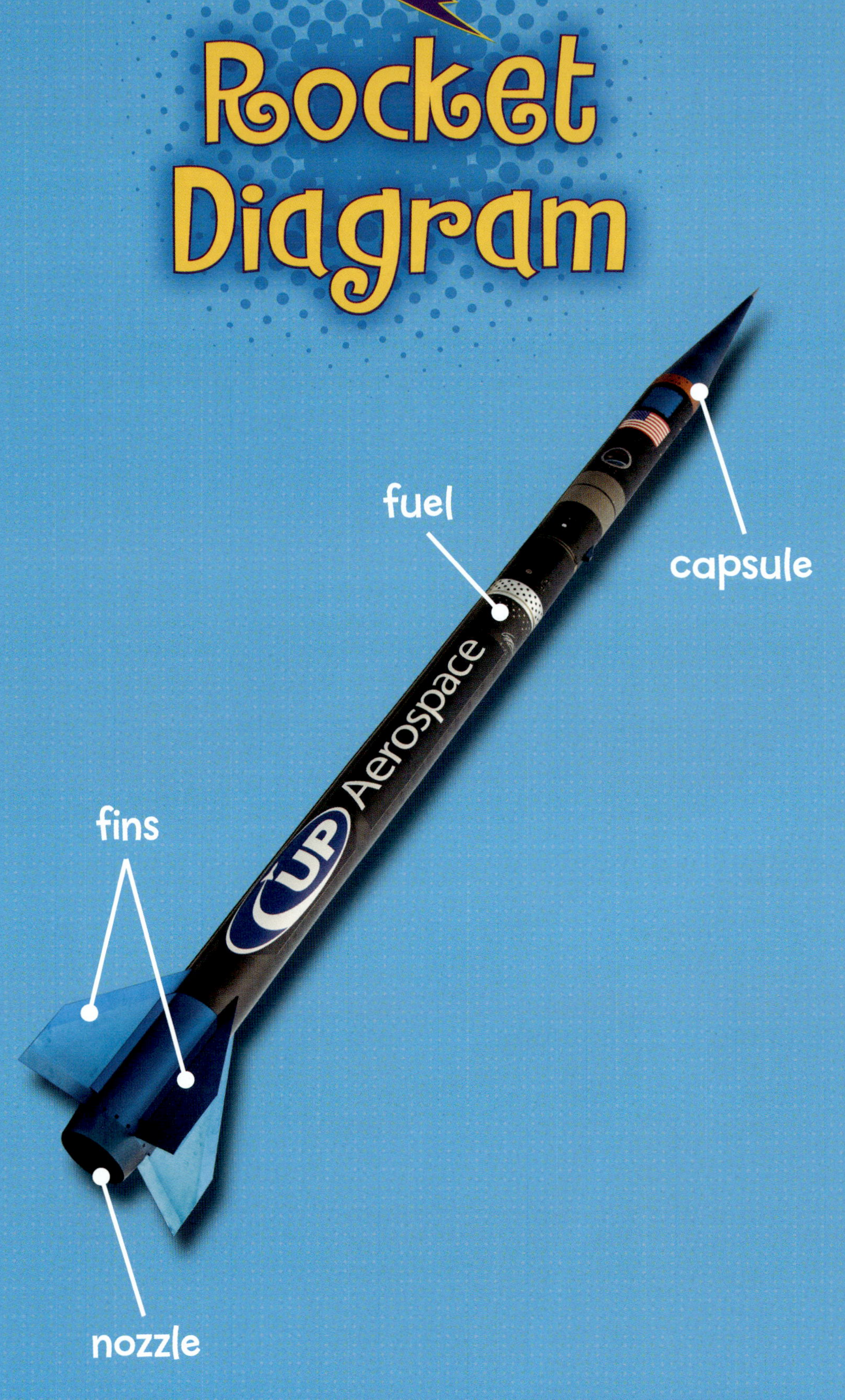

John Glenn Orbits Earth

On February 20, 1962, Friendship 7 launched on a rocket from Cape Canaveral, Florida. The spacecraft carried John Glenn. He became the first American to orbit Earth. Glenn orbited Earth three times before guiding the capsule into the North Atlantic Ocean for splashdown. Then a US Navy destroyer pulled the capsule onto the deck of the ship. A smiling John Glenn exited a hatch and was safe. The entire Friendship mission lasted four hours, fifty-five minutes, and twenty-three seconds.

Glossary

astronaut: someone who travels in space

capsule: the part of the rocket or spacecraft in which the crew travels

liftoff: the movement of a rocket or spacecraft as it rises from its launching pad

orbit: to travel around a planet, a moon, or the sun

payload: the equipment, satellite, crew, or cargo that is carried into space by a rocket

satellite: a spacecraft that is sent into orbit around a body in space

Learn More

Golusky, Jackie. *Space Exploration Robots.* Minneapolis: Lerner Publications, 2021.

Kington, Emily. *The Young Astronaut's Guide to Exploring Space.* Minneapolis: Hungry Tomato, 2021.

Kruesi, Liz. *Space.* Mankato, MN: Child's World, 2020.

NASA Science Space Place: Build a Bubble-Powered Rocket!
https://spaceplace.nasa.gov/pop-rocket/en/

NASA Science Space Place: Solar System
https://spaceplace.nasa.gov/menu/solar-system/

Time for Kids: One Giant Leap
https://www.timeforkids.com/g56/spacex-launch/

Index

Photo Acknowledgments

Image credits: United Launch Alliance, p. 4; NASA, pp. 5, 7, 10, 11, 20; FLHC 62/Alamy Stock Photo, p. 6; Aunt Spray/Shutterstock.com, p. 8; Bettmann/Getty Images, p. 9; NASA/Bill Ingalls, p. 12; courtesy of SpaceX, pp. 13, 14; NASA/JPL-Caltech/MSSS, p. 15; Aphelleon/Shutterstock.com, p. 16; 3Dsculptor/Shutterstock.com, p. 17; NASA Goddard Space Flight Center, p. 18; DAJ/Getty Images, p. 19.

Cover: 3Dsculptor/Shutterstock.com.